**WONDERS**
OF THE **WORLD**

Other books in the Wonders of the World series include:

Geysers
Icebergs
Mummies
Quicksand

# WONDERS
## OF THE **WORLD**

# Gems

Stuart A. Kallen

KIDHAVEN
PRESS™

THOMSON
™
GALE

San Diego • Detroit • New York • San Francisco • Cleveland
New Haven, Conn. • Waterville, Maine • London • Munich

© 2003 by KidHaven Press. KidHaven Press is an imprint of The Gale Group, Inc., a division of Thomson Learning, Inc.

KidHaven™ and Thomson Learning™ are trademarks used herein under license.

*For more information, contact*
KidHaven Press
27500 Drake Rd.
Farmington Hills, MI 48331-3535
Or you can visit our Internet site at http://www.gale.com

---

**LIBRARY OF CONGRESS CATALOGING-IN-PUBLICATION DATA**

Kallen, Stuart A. 1955–
    Gems / by Stuart A. Kallen.
        p. cm. — (Wonders of the world)
    ISBN 0-7377-1028-4 (hardback : alk. paper)
Summary: Discusses how gems are formed; where they are found; different types, sizes, shapes, and colors; mining gems; famous gems; and fake gems.
    1. Precious stones—Juvenile literature. [1. precious stones.] I. Kallen, Stuart A., 1955– II. Title.
    QE392.2 B64 2003
    553.8—dc21

                                              2002001269

---

Printed in the United States of America

# CONTENTS

# Gems from Rocks

**A** gem is a precious stone that has been cut and polished for use as jewelry or decoration. People have treasured gemstones for centuries because of their beauty, color, rarity, and hardness. And precious gems such as diamonds, rubies, and emeralds have long been considered the most valuable objects on Earth.

Most gemstones are formed deep within the earth in hot liquid rock called **magma**, similar to lava that flows from volcanoes. When the magma is pushed away from the hot center of the earth, it cools. When this happens water and minerals ooze out of the magma, creating hollow bubbles. Within these air pockets, or veins, hot water combines with the minerals to form large snowflakelike crystals that bond together to form gemstones.

Hot lava spews from a volcano. Gemstones are formed in magma, a hot liquid rock similar to lava.

## Diamonds

Diamonds are the most treasured of all gemstones. In addition to their sparkling beauty, they are also the hardest mineral on Earth. Diamond-tipped saws can cut through almost any material, including the hardest rocks.

Diamonds are formed under extreme pressure nearly 125 miles deep within the earth from pure carbon, a black, coal-like substance. Over the course of millions of years, they are pushed toward the surface by the flowing molten rock called **kimberlite**, which cools in long carrot-shaped formations that stick up slightly out of the ground.

Most diamonds are believed to be more than 3 billion years old—two-thirds as old as Earth itself. The first known diamond discovery was about twenty-four hundred years ago in India. The Indians called the diamonds *vajra*, or "thunderbolt," because the way the gems reflected light reminded them of lightning.

Before the fifteenth century, however, diamonds were not considered very valuable. This changed in 1456, when

Diamonds are believed to be almost as old as the earth.

stone cutters discovered how to cut flat, polished surfaces, called facets, into the gems. This process transformed diamonds from raw rocks into glittering treasures.

India continued to supply the entire world with diamonds until the eighteenth century, when supplies dwindled. In 1725 the stone was discovered in Brazil, which became a major supplier until 1866 when massive deposits were found in South Africa. Today diamonds are mined in twenty countries.

## Large and Valuable Diamonds

The largest diamond ever found is Cullinan, discovered in 1905 in the Premier Diamond Mine in Transvaal, South Africa. In its original form, Cullinan weighed an astonishing 3,106 **carats**, or about one and a half pounds. (A carat is a unit of measurement equal to 200 milligrams—142 carats equal 1 ounce.) In 1907 Cullinan was presented to King Edward of Britain, who had it divided into nine major gems and ninety-six smaller stones.

The world's largest cut diamond, called Cullinan I or the Great Star of Africa, was mounted on the British royal scepter, or staff. The second-largest stone cut from Cullinan is in the British imperial crown; it weighs 317 carats and is called Cullinan II or the Second Star of Africa. Two other large diamonds, Cullinan III and Cullinan IV, are in the queen's crown.

One of the most priceless diamonds is the 186-carat Koh-i-noor, or "Mountain of Light" diamond, owned by Indian royalty in the 1300s. The diamond changed hands several times and was finally given to England's

This man is holding the Cullinan diamond. At 3,106 carats it is the largest diamond ever found.

Queen Victoria in 1850. It is now on display with the British Crown Jewels in the Tower of London.

## Rubies

Rubies are the second-hardest stones after diamonds. And like diamonds, the glittering red stones have a long and colorful history.

Rubies are formed from the mineral corundum, which comes in many colors. The country of Burma is famous

A beautifully polished ruby sits atop an uncut ruby.

for producing clear, deep red rubies of the highest quality. Thailand produces dark red to brownish red rubies, and Africa is known for small purplish gems.

Rubies have been highly treasured for centuries and are believed to represent freedom, charity, dignity, and divine power. In ancient India they were known as drops of blood from the heart of Mother Earth.

## Emeralds

Although rubies and diamonds are the most valuable gems, emeralds have the longest history. Glittering green emeralds were cherished by the ancient Egyptians as long ago as 1300 B.C.—more than thirty-three

Emeralds are loved for their bright green color.

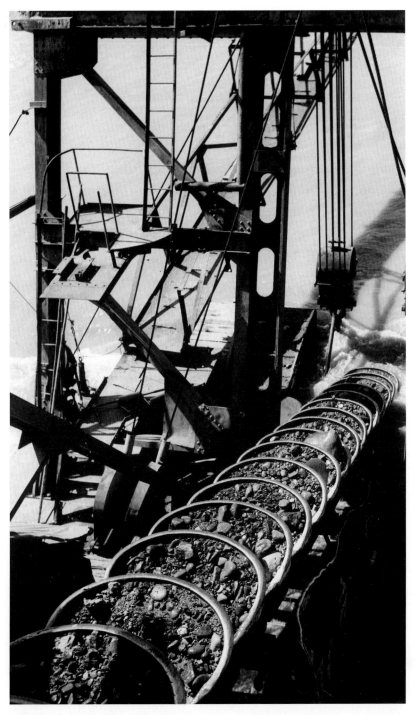

A machine sorts emeralds at a Colombia mine.

hundred years ago. The Egyptians depleted their emerald mines centuries ago, however, and the finest emeralds are now found around Muzo and Chivor in Colombia.

Emeralds belong to a family of six-sided crystals called **beryl** which, like diamonds, come in a variety of colors. Blue or blue-green beryl is called aquamarine, yellow beryl is called heliodor, and pink beryl is known as morganite. But the smallest, rarest beryl crystals are brilliant green emeralds, the most precious gems in the group. And the most prized emeralds are the color of dewy grass in spring.

## A Rainbow of Gems

Although emeralds, rubies, and diamonds are the most expensive stones, dozens of other gems are used for jewelry and decoration. These gemstones also represent the colors of the rainbow from pink and green tourmaline to blue and yellow topaz. And they are often used in place of their more expensive look-alikes. For example, red garnets are used instead of rubies. Green peridot may be substituted for emeralds. And inexpensive zircon has long been used in place of diamonds. Whether a stone is zircon or a diamond, the power and beauty of the gems may still give great pleasure to those who wear them.

# Gems from Plants and Animals

**A**lthough many gemstones are formed deep within the earth, some prized gems come from the world of plants and animals. These gems, such as pearls, coral, opals, and amber, are organic, meaning they come from living things. Although they are not as hard as diamonds or rubies, they have been valued for thousands of years because of their beauty.

## Pearls

Pearls are created by living creatures called **mollusks**. These animals, such as oysters and mussels, have hard shells. They may be found in the saltwater of the sea or in the freshwater of rivers and lakes. These creatures make many different colors of pearls, in shades of white, cream, and black, as well as purple, red, yellow, green, or

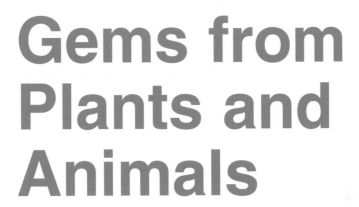

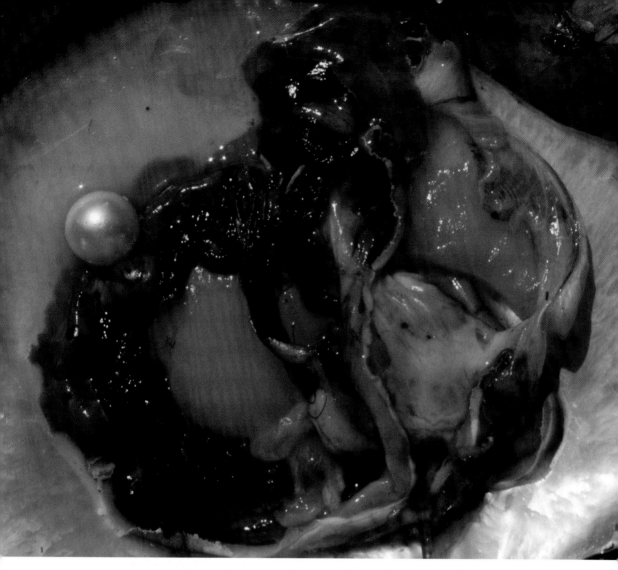

A gleaming pearl is produced inside this slimy oyster.

blue. Although any animal that produces a shell can make a pearl, the gems are very rare—only one in ten thousand mollusks makes a pearl.

Pearls are formed when an irritant, such as a food particle, becomes trapped in a mollusk's shell. The animal then coats the object with aragonite and conchiolin, materials it also uses to build its shell. Why this is done remains a mystery.

Pearl oysters can live for two hundred years, and oysters can grow pearls for fifty years, up to the size of a small egg. Pearls may be round or shaped like teardrops, seeds, eggs, pears, or flat-backed buttons. The most interesting and odd shapes are called baroque pearls. In fourteenth-century Europe, people used these oddly shaped baroque pearls to make decorative statues of fantastic creatures such as mermaids, centaurs, and dragons.

Pearls have always been valued for their shape, size, color, luster, and orient. (Luster is the sheen of the pearl's skin, and orient is the shine that comes from within.) One of the most famous pearls is the very large Peregrina, found in 1550 by an African slave on the coast of Panama. It has belonged to such famous historical figures as King Philip II of Spain and Mary Tudor of England. However, today the 27-carat pearl belongs to actress Elizabeth Taylor.

People have dived for pearls for centuries, but in recent times scientists have perfected ways of growing pearls inside mollusks. These gems are called cultured pearls. Using surgical equipment, skilled workers implant material inside the animals and wait decades for the mollusk to form the pearl. This unique process ensures that many pearls are available for necklaces, bracelets, earrings, and other jewelry.

## Coral

Like pearls, coral has been used in jewelry since prehistoric times. Coral is made of thin layers of a mineral called calcium carbonate, which comes from the protective skeletons of marine creatures. It is secreted over thousands of years by billions of tiny animals called coral polyps. Millions of coral polyps grow on top of the treelike remains of former colonies. These then form into massive **reefs** ten to forty-five feet under the sea. Most coral used in jewelry grows in the clear, warm shallow water along the shores of the Mediterranean and Red Seas. Coral has also been found in other warm coastal waters, including Hawaii, Japan, Malaysia, Australia, Ireland, and Mauritius.

Coral is made of tiny animals called coral polyps.

Since ancient times, red, orange, pink, and white coral has been harvested along these shores. The most valued colors are deep red, called ox blood, and pale pink, called angel skin.

Coral was popular with the ancient Greeks, who traded it with India and China. In Greek mythology, red coral is said to come from the drops of blood of Medusa, a snake-haired woman whose head was cut off. The Greeks carved coral into pictures of Medusa, and they wore it for magical protection from enemies.

Because coral grows very slowly, its continuing popularity for jewelry has put coral reefs in danger of extinction. Since the 1970s, conservation efforts have kept coral reefs from completely disappearing, but they remain under threat.

## Opals

Like coral, opals are made from the shells of microscopic creatures. Instead of forming in oceans, however, opals are made in very hot water under great pressure deep within the earth. Opals are mined very near the earth's surface in areas where ancient hot springs once flowed.

Opals shine in many colors, including the green of emeralds, the red of rubies, and the purple of the quartz stone amethyst. The multicolored reflection found in opals is called "play of color," and it is caused by diffracted light, the same effect that causes rainbows to appear in soap bubbles. With this display of color locked into every stone, it is little wonder that opals are called the "queen of gems."

Some of the world's largest opals have been found in Australia.

Although the Aztecs mined opals in Central America around five hundred years ago, today Australia is the top producer of the stone. The most expensive of the gems are black opals, which have a bright play of color. White opals display pastel colors. And fire opals have a slight yellow, orange, red, or brown background color.

A beautiful Hungarian opal called Orphanus was set in the crown of the Holy Roman Emperor, and it is still among the crown jewels of France. Nineteenth-century French emperor Napoléon gave Empress Joséphine an opal with brilliant red flashes, called the Burning of Troy. And a 77-carat opal is kept in the National Museum of Natural History in Paris.

Some of the largest opals in the world were discovered in the twentieth century. In 1954 a huge 203-carat opal was found in the Great Artesian Basin in Australia. It was cut and mounted in a necklace and earrings for the queen of England. Just two years later a gigantic 17,000-carat opal was found in Coober Pedy in Australia.

## Amber

Pearls and coral are formed from animals, but amber comes from the resin, or sap, of trees. This sap is millions of years old and has hardened beneath the surface of the earth, usually in lagoons, swamps, or other damp areas. Although it is used as a gemstone, amber is a plant-based substance that has changed little over the centuries. And because a very specific environment is needed to preserve amber, it is found in only twenty places on Earth. But almost all of the world's gem-quality amber—90 percent—is found along the coast of the Baltic Sea in Poland and Russia.

Amber is **translucent** to **transparent** and has been found in yellow, orange, red, brown, and whitish colors. Transparent amber sometimes appears green or blue because of the play of light through air bubbles trapped in

Amber comes from the fossilized sap produced by trees millions of years ago.

the ancient sap. Amber often hardens around plants, such as flowers, or insects, such as bees. Amber containing such interesting objects is highly valued for jewelry. And scientists are able to study this substance to understand the biology of creatures who lived long ago.

Amber buttons, beads, and pendants were made by Celts who lived along the Baltic Sea in 3700 B.C. They raked the amber from the bottom of the sea with long sticks or fished it out in nets when storms stirred the ancient gems to the surface. They traded the amber with the ancient Greeks and Romans for wine, oil, salt, silks, tea, bronze, and gold. In the Middle Ages, amber was called northern gold. Its softness made it easy to carve

These insects were trapped in sap that hardened to form amber.

into cameos and beads, and it was also used as a varnish for musical instruments and oil paintings.

Long before diamonds and rubies were cut and polished into priceless jewelry, organic gems such as pearls, coral, opals, and amber were considered treasures. And whether they were formed deep within the earth or found growing in the ocean, nature's wonders continue to delight and amaze.

CHAPTER
**THREE**

# Mining Gems

Diamonds, rubies, emeralds, and other jewels are treasured as precious jewelry, but mining for gems is hard, dirty, dangerous work. The earth does not give up its treasures easily, and miners use nearly every tool, including hatchets, picks, dynamite, and massive machines, to separate valuable gems from the worthless dirt, rock, and sand that surrounds them.

## Mining Rubies and Sapphires

Rubies and their close relatives, sapphires, account for more than half the world's sales in colored gemstones. These gems are mined in Myanmar, Thailand, Sri Lanka, Kenya, and the United States in Montana and North Carolina.

In ancient times, people mistakenly believed that rubies and sapphires grew under the ground like carrots or

This miner is being lowered into a mineshaft. Mining for gems is hard and dangerous work.

potatoes. They "planted" the gems like seeds, believing they would grow and multiply. Today, the search for these precious gems is conducted by miners who use picks and shovels to dig gem-bearing dirt out of the ground by hand.

In the Aqua Mine in Kenya, a crew of fifty men, using only picks and shovels, have dug a twisting, turning pit sixty feet deep over a two-acre area. The raw dirt from the dig is carried to a special washing plant, where a high-pressure water hose, much like a fire hose, shoots a powerful jet of water at the dirt. The water washes away the lighter dirt, clay, and sand, and leaves the heavier gravel and rock, along with the raw gemstones, which are separated out by hand.

Some sapphires are dug out of mines deep within the earth. At the Vortex Mine near Helena, Montana, eleven workers tunnel more than 250 feet below the surface of the earth, chipping away dirt and rock in search of what are known as cornflower blue Yogo sapphires. The mine is attached to a sixteen-foot-wide underground tunnel where trucks carry sapphire-rich ore to the surface for cleaning and sorting.

Mining tunnels are dark. Miners need equipment to help them see underground.

## Mining Emeralds

Like rubies and sapphires, emeralds are mined throughout the world, but many of the fine-quality gems come from eastern Brazil. At the Santa Teresinha Mine, about fifteen thousand workers have dug two hundred separate shafts into the ground to extract emeralds. These shafts are only three feet wide but may be anywhere from sixty to four hundred feet deep. The shafts extend to underground mines, where workers scrape out the precious stones with dynamite, hand picks, and jackhammers.

To get to these mines, workers are dropped down into the holes on old car tires that are raised and lowered by winches attached to thin steel cables. Workers

Gems hide deep in the walls of mines. Miners use large tools to get the gems out.

who take the dangerous three-minute rides are showered along the way with water that pours out of the rock walls. At the bottom of the pits, miners, wearing only shorts, labor in stifling heat and humidity.

## Clamoring for Riches

The country of Colombia lies on Brazil's western border, and some of the finest emeralds in the world come from the Muzo Mine, located sixty-five miles north of Bogotá. This mine consists of a huge pit where thousands of treasure hunters, known as *guaqueros*, gather to compete for gems. As the *guaqueros* wait, giant government-owned bulldozers push emerald-rich shale (rock formed from clay and mud) down into the pit where the treasure hunters use high-powered water hoses to separate the valuable gems from the black, powdery gravel. Thousands of hoses snake across the ground and every man in the pit is covered from head to toe with black, slippery muck from the wet shale dust. And the *guaqueros* consist of a dangerous mix of smugglers, outlaws, murderers, and thieves all clamoring for riches. Most miners carry knives and guns and murders happen often.

Half a world away, in Pakistan, miners must face different obstacles. Treasure seekers visiting the Gujar Kili Mine must hike for ninety minutes, crossing the swift-flowing Kotkai River three times before reaching their destination. When they finally reach an elevation of seven thousand feet above sea level, the miners must climb another three hundred feet straight up the cliffs above the river to get to the opening of the mine shaft.

## Gems Around the World

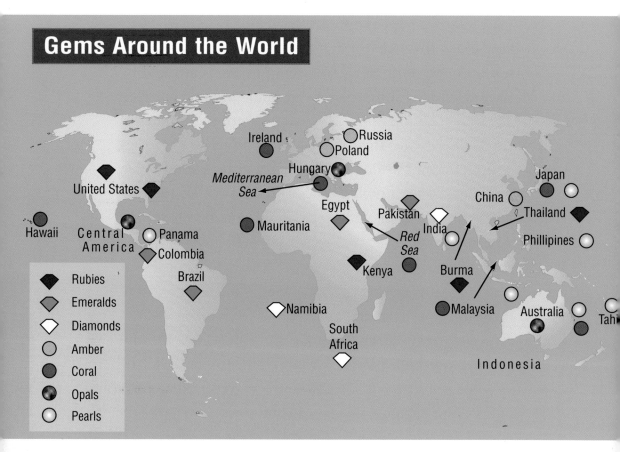

Ireland
Russia
Poland
Hungary
Mediterranean Sea
United States
Japan
China
Egypt
Thailand
Hawaii
Central America
Panama
Colombia
Mauritania
Pakistan
India
Red Sea
Phillipines
Brazil
Kenya
Burma
Namibia
Malaysia
Australia
Tah
South Africa
Indonesia

Rubies
Emeralds
Diamonds
Amber
Coral
Opals
Pearls

## Finding Diamonds

Although the mining of rubies, emeralds, and other gems has changed little over the years, diamonds have long been considered the most valuable stones. As a result, diamond miners have always invented new ways to scrape the stones from the earth.

As long ago as 1890, heavy industrial equipment was used to harvest diamonds at the Kimberly mines in South Africa. Huge steam-powered engines used steel ropes to drop buckets one thousand feet into the ground. Each bucket could pull nearly ten thousand pounds of kimberlite to the surface every thirty seconds.

Today, massive trucks are used to haul the kimberlite, which has been blasted with dynamite, out of enormous open pits. The gem-bearing gravel is crushed by huge machines and processed to remove the kimberlite and leave the diamonds. Because diamonds are heavier than gravel, cone-shaped washing pans are used to separate the gems from the surrounding dirt and gravel. These pans flood the raw ore with water while swirling blades stir up lighter material. Heavy diamonds sink to

Very large equipment is used to mine for diamonds. Here a truck works to move the sand that covers diamond-rich gravel.

the bottom of the cone and are pushed out through a small hole in the bottom of the pan. This process removes 99 percent of the waste and the remaining muddy ore may then be treated in one of two ways.

The first method, a long plank of wax-covered wood, known as the grease table, has been used since the nineteenth century. Diamonds stick easily to substances such as beeswax or paraffin. Grease tables are covered with this wax, and when the muddy ore is poured on the tables, the

After the diamond gravel is brought inside, it goes through large machines that extract the diamonds.

gems stick. The wax is then scraped off the grease table and melted into liquid. The diamonds are removed with a strainer.

A newer, high-tech method involves X rays, which make diamonds sparkle in an unusually bright manner. As the diamond-bearing ore is illuminated by an X-ray machine, an electronic device can "see" the diamonds. This device triggers an air jet to blow the gems into a bin. Like a grease table, this method removes massive quantities of waste. About 250 tons of kimberlite has to be processed in order to find a single one-carat diamond.

The most advanced mining methods are practiced with ships using giant drills to dig under the ocean floor. In southwestern Africa, off the coast of Namibia, ships such as the *Debmar Pacific* employ seventeen-foot-wide drill bits that sink holes three hundred feet under the surface of the South Atlantic. Machines suck up nearly one hundred tons of drilled material an hour, twenty-four hours a day, seven days a week. This raw material is never touched by human hands. Instead it is automatically sent through a series of sieves, whirling separators, and X-ray machines. The final product is sealed in metal cans that are airlifted by helicopter to mining sales offices on land. Mining ships such as the *Debmar Pacific* remove nineteen thousand carats of diamonds from the ocean every month—about twenty-six carats an hour.

As long as people buy diamonds, miners are willing to work long hours to find these elusive stones. Every year about 120 million carats of diamonds—about

Boats use drills to mine for diamonds under the ocean floor.

twenty-four tons—are mined from the earth. Although these diamonds would fill only a single dump truck, they are worth more than $50 billion when sold as jewelry. Because it costs only $2 billion to extract these gems, there are fortunes to be made in diamond mining.

# CHAPTER FOUR

# The World's Most Famous Gems

**M**illions of gems have been mined over the centuries, and most were passed along to buyers and jewelers unnoticed. But a few emeralds, rubies, and diamonds are so large, or so unusual, that they have become world famous. And some of these gems, such as the Hope Diamond, are so sought-after that they have long stories, often filled with curses, mystery, and murder.

## The Curse of the Hope Diamond

The blue Hope Diamond is one of the most famous gems in history. The giant stone weighed more than 112 carats when it was originally mined in India in the 1600s. But owners of the Hope Diamond, over the centuries, have had an unusual run of bad luck, so much so that it is said to be cursed.

The Hope Diamond is on display at the Smithsonian. Some people believe that the Hope Diamond is cursed.

# Stolen from a Hindu God?

According to legend, the Hope Diamond was originally stolen from a Hindu god who put a curse on the stone. It was then sold to French king Louis XIV in 1668, who called it "Blue Diamond of the Crown." It was passed along to French queen Marie Antoinette, who was killed in 1793 during the French Revolution. The diamond was stolen from the French royal palace and disappeared for decades, then mysteriously surfaced in London in 1830. By this time the gem had been cut down to its present 44.5-carat oval shape. It was purchased for $90,000—a huge sum at the time—by Henry Hope, who gave the diamond its name. Hope's heirs inherited the stone when he died, but they suffered financial difficulties and were forced to sell it.

The Hope Diamond was purchased by a European prince, who gave it to an actress in the French theater. The prince later shot the actress in a jealous rage. The stone was later sold to a wealthy Greek merchant who soon died with his family when his car plunged over a cliff. Later, Turkish sultan Abdul-Hamid II obtained the stone, but he owned it for only a few months when a military revolt stripped him of power in 1909.

American heiress Evalyn Walsh McLean was the first American to own the Hope Diamond. McLean purchased it for $180,000 from world-famous jeweler Pierre Cartier after it had been set into a necklace with sixty-two white diamonds. McLean could not escape the stone's curse, however. Two of her children died in an accident and her husband later went insane.

In 1947, after McLean died, the Hope Diamond was purchased by New York jeweler Harry Winston, who donated it to the Smithsonian Institution in 1958. Today this priceless gem remains at the Smithsonian in a burglarproof case. More than 3 million people a year gaze upon its beauty at the museum.

## Famous Rubies and Emeralds

Few gems can match the fame of the Hope Diamond, but several rubies are treasured for their size and beauty. One particularly famous ruby is surrounded by twenty-six diamonds in the gold coronation ring of English kings.

Some of the most famous rubies are found in this British coronation ring.

Other precious rubies are found in museums through-out the world. The 105-carat Anne of Brittany Ruby is found in the famous Louvre in Paris, France. The British Museum of Natural History houses the astounding 167-carat Edwardes Ruby. This stone was named for Major General Sir Herbert Benjamin Edwardes, who fought for the British in India in the nineteenth century.

The United States is home to several renowned rubies. The Smithsonian houses the 137-carat Rosser Reeves Ruby, and the American Museum of Natural History in New York City has the 100-carat Edith Haggin de Long Ruby.

One of the largest emeralds in the world is the Mogul Emerald, discovered around 1695. This massive stone weighs more than 217 carats and is almost four inches high. One side is inscribed with prayers; the other side is decorated with beautiful carved flowers. When this rare emerald was sold at auction in London in 2001, an anony-mous buyer paid $2.2 million for the gem.

## Globe of Jewels

One of the most incredible gem-studded objects is an eighteen-inch round globe of the world. This depiction of the planet contains fifty-one thousand gems. Countries are laid out in red rubies set in gold, while the sea is made from green emeralds. The entire globe is set in a circular gold ring encrusted with diamonds. The jeweled globe was first made for the Great Mogul of India, but was stolen in 1739 by the Persian conqueror Nadir Shah. Today it is part of the crown jewels of Iran and is displayed in Tehran.

# Famous Fakes

Some famous jewels that have been revered for centuries are not really the precious gems they were once believed to be. For example, the Talisman of Charlemagne, housed in a French museum, contains two stones said to be large sapphires. Jewelers who have examined this ninth-century relic have recently discovered that it is really made from pale, blue glass over common quartz crystal.

And, some very large red gemstones once believed to be rubies are not really rubies at all. Instead, they are actually stones called **spinels**—ruby-red rocks formed from minerals such as magnesium and aluminum.

Charlemagne owned jewels he thought were real, but were later discovered to be fake.

Once a year, a jeweler examines and cleans every gem on the Imperial State Crown. Each jewel is carefully inspected for authenticity.

In England the 170-carat Black Prince's Ruby, worn in battle by English king Henry V in 1415, is really a red spinel. Although this stone is displayed with the British Crown Jewels in the Tower of London, it has much less value than a real ruby.

Another famous fake ruby is found in the nineteenth-century armlet, or arm band, once owned by Queen

Therese of Bavaria. The rubies in the armlet, now displayed in a Bavarian castle, are seriously scratched. Scratched rubies are highly unusual because they are second only to diamonds in hardness. Experts have concluded that the rubies worn by Queen Therese are really made from glass.

It is possible the queen never knew of this fraud. Researchers speculate that in one royal ring, the real stones may have been stolen by relatives who covered their crime by replacing them with glass worth much less than the original gems.

## A World of Gems

From the blue Hope Diamond to the half-carat stones sold at jewelry stores in shopping malls, gems are ancient gifts from the earth. They have been revered for centuries and are valued by rich and poor alike. With their dazzling sparkle and beautiful appearance, there is little doubt that rubies, pearls, diamonds, emeralds, and other stones will keep their value for a long time to come.

# Glossary

**beryl:** Six-sided crystals that form the base of various colored gems such as emeralds, aquamarine, heliodor, and morganite.

**carat:** Unit of measurement equal to 200 milligrams each.

**kimberlite:** Hardened magma containing diamonds.

**magma:** Hot liquid rock.

**mollusks:** Thin-shelled creatures with soft bodies such as snails, clams, oysters, and mussels.

**reefs:** Chains of rocks or coral.

**spinels:** Ruby-red rocks formed from minerals such as magnesium and aluminum.

**translucent:** Clear, transparent.

**transparent:** Easily seen through.

# For Further Exploration

Emma Foa, *Gemstones*, New York: DK Publishing, 1997. The history of gemstones told with simple text and many pictures.

Ian Mercer, *Gem Stones*. New York: Gloucester Press, 1987. A look at gems and their long history.

Christopher Pellant, *Collecting Gems & Minerals: Hold the Treasures of the Earth in the Palm of Your Hand*. New York: Sterling Publications, 1998. How gems and minerals are formed, how they have been used throughout history, and where to look for them.

R.F. Symes and R.R. Harding, *Crystals & Gems*. New York: Knopf, 1991. A colorful book with many photos and drawings tracing the history and science of gems.

# Index

# Picture Credits

# About the Author

Stuart A. Kallen is the author of more than 150 nonfiction books for children and young adults. He has written extensively about Native Americans and American history. In addition, Mr. Kallen has written award-winning children's videos and television scripts. In his spare time, Stuart A. Kallen is a singer/songwriter/guitarist in San Diego, California.